THE SUDDEN COUNTRY

poetry by

David Mills

MAIN STREET RAG PUBLISHING COMPANY
CHARLOTTE, NORTH CAROLINA

Copyright © 2013 David Mills
Cover photography: Sunset near Agate Beach, Oregon
   by M. Scott Douglass
Author photo by:

Acknowledgments:

The Pedestal Magazine: "Fool's Gold"
Rattapallax: "The Shadow of Language"
Transitions (Harvard University Dubois Institute): "A Parable of Skillets"
Brooklyn Rail: "Moon in a Blue Once," "The Translation of Faile St."
www.Pennsounds.com: "The Shadow of Language"
The Literary Review Fairleigh Dickinson University: "Sealed with a Kiss," "Elmina."
African-American Review: "This Murdered Earth," "Haiku"
Aloud: Voices from the Nuyorican Poets Café: "G-Men in the Pines"
Margie: "I, Tina."
Obsidian III: "Sealed with a Kiss"
The Ringing Ear: "Three-The Hard Way"
Aspeers: "Illiterate Fish"
Warpland: "Cabo Corso"
Black Renaissance Noir: "Syllables and Lipstick," "Rio De Ja Vu No," "Poem No. 35," "Poem No. 22," "Norma & Bubba," "Rime Royal," "Blues"
Drum Voices Revue: "Elmina"
New Rain: "El Norte"
New Observations: "Back Space: Return"
Dark Symphony: "Flight 990," "Nosey"
Reverie: "Do I Believe in G-d, No Does G-d Believe in Me"
Peepal Tree Press: Jubilaton: An Anthology celebrating Jamaica's 50th anniversary of Independence): "The Sudden Country," "17"

Library of Congress Control Number: 2013935418

ISBN: 978-1-59948-422-8

Produced in the United States of America

Main Street Rag
PO Box 690100
Charlotte, NC 28227
www.MainStreetRag.com

Do you understand the stillness...
Langston Hughes

Contents

The Sudden Country 1

Part I

Three the Hard Way 7
I, Tina 13
Do I Believe 15
Illiterate Fish 16
Block Island Cemetery 19
Syllables and Lipstick 21
The Bone Labyrinth 22
G-Men In the Pines 24
Sad, But True: A Duet 25
Truth Is 26

Part II

Medium Evening 31
Fool's Gold .34
Back Space: Return 37
Elmina 40
Cabo Corso .42
This Murdered Earth 43
Sealed With a Kiss 44
University of Robben Island 45
Out of My System 46
Flight 990 47

Part III

Poem No. 22 51
Haiku 52
Blues 53

Rime Royale 54
Poem No. 35. 56
Norma & Bubba 57

Part IV

As if Joy. 61
Nosey 64
Sweet 16 66
17 68

Part V

Moon in a Blue Once 73
So Little of Holland 74
The Shadow of Language 75

Part VI

A Parable of Skillets 79
Rio De Ja Vu No 80
Easter in Rio 81
Monday's at Martha's Vineyard 82
Abuela's Dreams. 83
El Norte. 86

Notes 88

THE SUDDEN COUNTRY

(Jamaica, West Indies)

We loped down Standfast to the riot and whirr
of Brown's Town market. Between chipped
columns and beneath a corrugated roof, Dad,
like Uncle—who was paid to frisk produce—
fingered tamarinds and the sweet stink of mango.

Content, Dad flagged down a van. Slid the side
door open. The sound like teeth biting a crisp June
Plum. I climbed in, and my sandal slapped a puddle's
oily rainbow. I leaned my head against a tinted window:
my thighs met by the prickle and balm of broken

upholstery and exposed padding. The driver—vexed
by shiftless GMC Rallys, Dodge Sportsmans, ankles
and insteps stalking soccer balls, and the occasional mangy
dog—yelled: a 50,000-year-old grouse. A sound one could trail
like Theseus' string back into the driver's maw, back through

labyrinths and passages to the first keen of human speech.
With the heel of his palm, he slammed the steering wheel
as if this were a karate class: the push and penetrate,
the technique and burst of adolescent pine board.
Beneath the tires, coconut husks and shards of Red

Stripe crunched and popped. He sped off. Everyone
on board was pinched tight as a pack of menthol
Matterhorns. The V-8's hack and flatulence did not
keep him from playing chicken with other vans.
What of driving on a thoroughfare's left side?

A soft-voiced woman turned my way: "No worry,
I know G-d, and he's sitting next to me." Her thick,
lower lip, bordered: the sudden country chapped,
chocolate; the back country somewhere between
crimson and mauve. We passed mango trees, rockets

of corn. Had it been Saturday, Uncle would have carted
us the nine miles to Cousin Lindy's; would have whisked
us in his 1950s' white Zephyr: its pristine chassis always
made me feel like I was buckled in a cirrus cloud's plush
back seat. Made me forget the steering wheel was on

a car's passenger side. The van's window latch pulled up
and pushed out. A breeze: thick, warm as a bottle of Irish
Sea Moss orphaned on Granny's verandah. I held a gift
of Kelly's Strawberry Syrup in one hand, guzzled a bottle
of kola champagne with the other. A gravel-voiced DJ

yammered on the radio. No matter the mother, the tongue
is always pink speech; succinct meat; evidence of an icy's
escape plan; or song's stained carpet. The WRJR jock spun
Land of my Birth—a melody that seasoned that August's
air. I could not remember the verses, wondered why

words seemed to be so much about the mind, the mouth,
but melodies hummed in the chest's heaving grotto. I tagged
along with Donaldson's zesty, skipping rhythm, sang
the hook: "This is the Land of my Birth. This is Jamaica, my
Jamaica…" That second syllable in Jamaica—that *ma*—made

the front of my tongue slope downward, so the lyrics might quicken
like a van hurtling toward Runaway Bay. The front tire punched
a pothole, and my head nearly hit the roof of the Ford E-Series
while lyrics banged off the roof of my mouth. The honk
honking drove my forefingers to my ears. And as if an amp

had been lodged in my skull, my head resounded with song.
Oh, how I offered my twelve-year-old self to that chorus:
the delicious again and again of it. That summer of '78,
my mouth felt like a stadium of swaying Jamaicans, heads
held high: Donaldson's song an anthem. This, so soon

after that once unthinkable April where Nesta convinced
Manley and Edward to come together in a *feel all right*.
Sixteen years earlier, the October after the island's, Dad
had gained his independence and citizenship with winter.
Back then, I was not even a grunt in my father's underwear.

But on that August afternoon as the van shook like a drunk's
stomach, there were no *light throughs* nor *lest wes;* no songs
sounding as if a tongue had to snap to attention before words-
dry cleaned and spit shined—marched from a mouth. The tongue,
the palate: pink planets. Words: meteors born to burn beyond

these worlds, to escape spit's inner space and enter an atmosphere
incandescent with meaning, where syllable and sense gleam
and fizzle, slam and vanish, or fall silent, down like a wad
of bubble gum hawked from the driver's mouth. Gum stuck
to the van's floor mat; gum itching for the driver to open

his trap and bark in patois; gum that will gaze at the roof
of that driver's mouth—that blunt, pink planet—and though
dented by memory and teeth, gum that will sense that it is
the abandoned shadow of that celestial palate. That that hawking
could have only happened in August when the Perseid reach

their peak, when fragments are not just stone, but shards
of English broken and ancient; are sentences, fleeced of either
subject or verb, hurtling through space. A tattered green, gold
and black flag dangled from the van's rearview mirror. Yet
there was no pomp, no circumstance, just a man—my father

—whose mouth often took twelve months to commit to a grin.
But on this afternoon in the second month that starts with *A*,
Dad's mouth was open, gap-toothed, brimming with glee
and song. One blood, one love: his mouth and mine, passengers in a van whose driver believed traffic was a martial art,

who had faith in how the heel of a palm inaugurates the blat
of a horn: who praised his steering wheel's kiai when it pummeled
Donaldson's tenor. Still, a few miles from *Runaway*, he ran
headlong into road, which dipped and curved like the side
of a tongue when it's been asked to keep the promise of song.

PART I

Love is so short forgetting is so long

—Pablo Neruda

THREE THE HARD WAY

After Zora Neale Hurston's Their Eyes Were Watching G-d

I

Grandma didn't want me
to hoe from can't see
in the morning till can't see
at night. It wasn't Logan

Killicks she wanted me to marry.
It was protection. It was 60 acres
of cotton and sweat. It was walking
in the house and waiting for love

to begin. Noticing poems didn't
grow in his mouth; his fingers
sobering up in my long,
black hair just two months

after our tongues came
closer than words. It was his
long, flat head and fatback.
I was a mystery. I wanted

to want him. Didn't want him to
do all the wantin.' Didn't want him
to tell me to chop wood. Shoot,
the earth drinks piss and perfume

just the same. So I cut his coffee,
fried the hoe-cake, glazed the sow
belly. I ain't gonna ache. Ain't
gonna wait. Gone.

II

Sittin' on the porch: Eatonville. Sun
light sneaking through the slats, taking
a breather after traveling a spell.
Citified Georgia Joe gone. I sent
my feelings to the funeral. Some

think I'm the reason. *Questionizin*
him. But I had an inside
and an outside, knew how
to hang them in different
closets. Seal Brown Joe,
mayor of Eatonville. Mouth

so big the Mississippi shivered
when he spoke—we lived in Florida:
You ain't got no more business
wid uh plow than a hog has got
wid uh holiday. I couldn't be

around the gum grease, had to
rub tongues with the high muckety
-mucks, sit with my wrists and hands
folded while he shoved rules down
my throat. Wouldn't let me get

in the conversations on
the porch; wouldn't let me
roll in the laughter, would
breathe for me if he could
wedge his breath in my nostrils.

Portly when I met him, now fat
waddled across his ribs. But he
always insulting me: *You old
as Methuselah, rump hanging
to your knees.* My calves were fat

with answers I had kept to myself.
But one day I peeled back
my tongue: "Joe you pull down
your britches and the wind covers
its eyes." The men's laughter made
his ankles explode. He pointed

his stogie, that fat finger of spinach,
then lifted his left hand so high
the sky flinched: *Ah see one
thing and understand ten.*

You see ten and understand one.
There was silence, the quiet
of knives. I yanked that doo-
rag—his skull cuff—off
my head, let my hair tickle

my hips on the way home. Joe moved
downstairs. Love left the bedroom,
sat in the parlor, made small talk
with the customers. Mississippi
didn't get the jitters no more.

III

I am coffee. I am cream. Mrs. Turner
say I'm a featured woman, ain't got no
liver lips and flat nose. But I'm in love

with the coo in midnight. Teacake
I'm afraid of misunderstanding more
than death, waking up in a bed dizzy

with sweet talking and sex. My
fingernails, my breasts, the ball
of my foot is one slow love

song only you know how to sing.
You learned me ecstasy; you
learned me jealousy. Love

so good it throbbed when I seen muscle
-butt Nunkie out in the cotton
trying to grab that giggle

'tween your legs. Trying to snatch
my laughter. I bought it, paid
for it, spread the wrinkled wings

between my legs for it. Lake
Okechobee's bosom spilling out
her bra, muddy jugs big enough

to feed the Mississippi. In those
waters, some dog sharpened
its canines on a hurricane. You

brandished your knife, croaked
that mutt, but not before that dog
chewed the swagger in your left cheek.

IV

How do you aim a gun
at love? Is it as simple
as fishing and checkers? Half
G-d's sip wine and buttercups.

Real G-d's drink blood. Teacake,
I see you kissing that pillow.
*How come you can't sleep
with me, woman?* His tongue

flopping like a jittery sock. He
choking on a cup of water that's soft
and wrong, thinking he reaching
for a pinch of the river. *I need*

a quart of coon dick. I'd lick
the moon's ear if it would
save you Teacake. *What
you want in that bedroom?*
That pistol under the pillow.

A six-shooter with five hongry
chambers, we only gonna have
one meal this evening. Fear
and hope. Click. Hope

and fear. Click. How do I
aim a gun at love? *Teacake*
there's a possum struttin'
'cross your eyelashes. I whipped

up the Winchester, winced and shot.
He poured his body, that lanky love
song, into my lap. Why I had to
put a bullet in the music, sugar?

If you'll 'low me, Lord, I'm
gonna unbutton this house,
let Teacake's final breath crawl
out the window. Bootyny! Sop

De Bottom! Coodemay! Stew Beef!
SSSh. This sadness is animal,
killing me through Teacake. Baby,
you loved me in blue. I couldn't wear

it right now. I looked down.
Mrs. Turner would say I was
staring at the dark. But my eyes,
my eyes were watching G-d.

I, TINA

For Tina Turner

Allegro

I am Nutbush, honeysuckle, a mile
long burp of pickaninny twists.

I am live wire, black pepper, toe jam
you drink with Kahlua. I am rag

time, Roaring 20's, the small talk
between his fingers and a baby

grand. I am a whisper. You know I loved
him through music. I wasn't his type

of woman. He wasn't my type
of man. I've always liked 'em high

yellow. But one night we were
driving home and he made me

straddle the steering wheel.
Ike and Bo Didley on KJKJ,

slipping in my sticky.
It was like doing it

with your brother. Of course,
I fell in love. I didn't know

I was a one-way ticket
out of my own teeth.

Adagio

I am a bowl of razor blades, spinning,
                              peeling the skin off my legs.
I am the black eye of his storm. He was
                              like out of nowhere: Pow!
I am the basic beat up: club
                              dates and cancelled fantasies.

Presto

He is a nose icy with coke.
I am licking the Lord's Prayer

off a limo's glass. I am a scream
limping toward my own teeth. I am nothing

but shimmies and lyrics to this man;
a cheek that turns as he pulls out

before he considers the wet
suggestion I had offered him.

I am silent as he unscrews
hallelujah from some

groupie's spit.
I am one of many

all of us nine months
of his music.

DO I BELIEVE IN G-D, NO DOES G-D BELIEVE IN ME?

You see my whole life is tied up to unhappiness 'cause it's the only for real thing I know.
　　　　　　　　　　　　　　　　—Nikki Giovanni

My womb is silent. The rest
of my body a foreign language:
kidneys that speak Yiddish;
a ring of bones that whisper
Kickapoo; a mystery. Twice
I have outlived my children. I can't
imagine adopting when all I wanted
was the suck and swallow, for either
of them to have turned their mouths
to my milk. But now my nipples are bricks—
large and dark as midnight; my womb a paper
bag crumpled and tossed from a cross-town
bus. G-d, all I wanted was a first word's puny
hallelujah. I remember my belly, that voluptuous gust,
the almost nine months—both times. But those breezes
have since withered. Now when my lips are torn apart,
words like *rage, hate* and *betrayal* fly from my mouth:
long *A* sounds that have me wheezing with morning
sickness; long *A* sounds that have me flirting
with the notion of opening an agency
with one toddler named G-d
who I'll put up for adoption;
long *A* sounds that have
made me think.
Twice.

ILLITERATE FISH

As the Gypsy Kings snap and tickle starlight, your feet
summon tapioca ghosts from *Lodz'* dust. The way doves
dress themselves in glass, after mistaking a window

pane for a cloud, my pupils confuse your sable bangs
for condors streaking above your eyes' azure skies. We serve
each other words as Pavel becomes the net in our singles

ping-pong match. *May I buy you a drink?* The whites
of Pavel's eyes back spin with your volley: "*barze dobje*,
why won't he ask to make love?" *Pavel don't ruin this.*

May I drink you by the light crawling out of the moon? Due
to his tipsy fibs, I place a word on Pavel's tongue, esplanade (v):
to attempt an explanation while drunk. Another,

flatulence (n): the emergency vehicle I commandeer,
which scrapes Pavel up once he's plastered by a steam
roller for thwarting my chances. This way he wouldn't

have to get around with a lymph (v): to walk with a lisp.
At a bar, you mix potions that unbutton tongues, pour
me upstairs. The angel twirling beneath the slick tent

our tongues make pinwheels backwards through time.
Our first kiss flew to Iceland, then smooched the inseam
between Bavaria and the country this kiss was headed for.

In *Sublice*, a Polish whistle stop, this kiss had to show its pass
-port three times. Apparently, this kiss was unrecognizable
with its duds: a moustache, brown eyes. Dressed in darkness,

this kiss wondered how the night worked its way into two
men's shoulders, like snow kneads its way into stone?
This kiss noticed people staring as it boarded a 10:07

train to *Lodz*. What's so unusual about a pair of lips kicking
back in the dining car? I wonder if you now know this
kiss, inches from your lips, hums with all this history. I

carve your bone-black outfit from your skin. My tongue
appraises your creamy, naked landscape. I'll never have
to teach you words like: flabbergasted (vt): to give up all

hope of ever having a flat tummy. As your hands clamp
down on my BVDs, I teach you your first word in English,
circumvent (n): the opening in the front of boxer shorts.

Wearing a condom, I slowly enter a foreign country
where words like oyster (n)—a person who sprinkles
his conversation with Yiddish—are uttered. As we scrub

each other's skin 'til daylight creeps, you repeatedly coo:
barze dobje. I cum, white chocolate anoints the roof of my
Trojan. *Ni spac, ni spac*. You break night; but moments

later you're yanking on me like a poodle too stupid
to follow the edicts in your leash. We spoon in Pavel's
bed with a yellow Polish-English dictionary snug

between us: our Berlitz Berlin Wall; east to west, woman
to man, communicating 'til the sea that purrs between us
burns and flees. We glisten with brief interludes of, *You*

tired? Or answering the door, you learn <u>negligent (adj)</u>:
a condition where you absent-mindedly get the door
in your nightie. I now know *barze dobje* means very good.

But back on the backside of the Atlantic, my heart is two
question marks staring at each other but afraid to come
closer, afraid that no dictionary is equipped to translate

two
   tongues
      that
         once
            danced
               like
                  illiterate
                     fish.

BLOCK ISLAND CEMETERY

inches past
the cemetery's entrance, the first marker:
Simon 10/10/1856—my birthday; next:
Celia, Simon's wife, April 22nd—days
before yours. Should I unearth the earth
beneath Simon's headstone? Should you
do the same to Celia's? Should I baffle
the roots nursing the emerald world; pry
his coffin's cedar lid where decomposition

shredded the skin's seven vestibules; Simon's right
humerus: a curtain rod twisted to open his ribs:
a decedent's Venetian blinds. No longer vein
nor atrium; no longer ventricle nor artery,
Simon's heart (tufted cloud, puce cumulus,
pump of nothing) drifts in a sky's obstinate darkness.
What might the world beneath this pious hill

long to say after you've tossed aside all
but one pillow? Its sable and magenta
case striped like an nearly-extinct Bengal
Tiger; after **Christina**, from a world
that hangs on your cream walls, obeys
Andrew and gives her back to the 20th
century; away from where—below the waist

and beyond a walnut and merlot frame—
we burn; and **Christina's** body—housed
in Wyeth's mounting—starts its painted
betrayal. After **Christina** faces the 18th
century: a tempera field emptied of its
emptiness: a tawny hill, an unmarked
boneyard, a seafarer's Cushing home;
after you've perched both calves on

my clavicles. And at the hint of my entry rest
a forearm across your thighs. There've been
moments in those half-lights where I've drifted
over your hazel eyes and sensed our intimacy
was not a now but a then, a fissure, a withered
century. Where you and I were you and I
and somehow time has reacquainted us:
                                                disguised.

SYLLABLES AND LIPSTICK

Love is so short, forgetting is so long.
—Pablo Neruda

Your lips silk pillows where my dreams rest.
Where do conversations end and kisses begin
when syllables and lipstick wear the same breath?

My dreams are six seas where I'm seldom wet.
Your breast: black bass swimming in your skin.
Your lips: silk pillows where my dreams rest.

Sometimes silence has gotten up, has left,
when our mouths are crowded with sin, since
syllables and lipstick wear the same breath.

At night when the moon's an uninvited guest,
and your curtains become a womb for the wind:
your lips silk pillows where my dreams rest.

At daybreak most stars tend to speak of death
as *Helios* cracks the light in their ribs.
Now syllables and sunlight share the same breath.

Our tongues are the ways our mouths confess
to the voluptuous trouble we're in.
Your lips: silk pillows where my dreams rest,
where syllables and lipstick wear the same breath.

THE BONE LABYRINTH

I

Between April Fool's and April 4th; before Final Fours and Easter eggs; sans purple robe or crown of thorns you left. No wine and myrrh; no place of skulls; no linen silence; your 9th hour: 5:40 a.m. Friday, weeping on a hospice's pinewood floor. Dawn, an ointment of vinegar and plain chant. Is there a Golgotha's why? An ecclesiastical what have you? A stone's forsaken? A me among equals? What we know is what we don't. 4/4 time: Grandma's day of cake and candle; Martin's Memphis: a blood-soaked balcony; in twenty-ten—Jesus' resurrection. Had that Friday been more than good and kin to kind, you would've been perched in front of a plasma canvas; glued to West Virginia/Duke—the college from your momma's Carolina: goosefoot and knotweed; jimson and Kitty Hawk. But Prince of Peace, don't double down. Even if an athlete's body is a congregation of gristle and dream; free throws—prayer; the net a soft, braided heaven used to practice this petition: flick the hollow above the wrist, crouch, rise, and arc a tangerine rock—that Spalding rind that abandoned pulp and seed for air. My G-d; my aunt; my Mt. Eden *Eloi* up on 1744 Clay Ave—lop off that final 4, exit the D train at 174th Street.

II

Jerry—your German Shepherd—wet nostrils throbbing like a mugger's heart. Whenever he barked my ten-year-old blood hid in my sacrum and sacroiliac: (bones that flare like a provoked Cobra.) *When you gon' get married?* You teased. Lit Virginia Slims; gravel laughter. *You'd come a long way baby.* With each drag, the tobacco went from caramel to ash. *Bring me a cold one, David!* Flamboyant as Dali's moustache, the Schaefer beer logo—two ears of barley with stems that kiss and curve up and away. The can's bottom read: "Store in a cool place." So I placed 12 fl. oz of cool in your palm. When you popped that pull tab—it exhaled a pinched sneeze. You tilted the brew to your lips. Nursed and slurped from that absence shaped like an uvula; basked in the beer's growl and *Ahh*. Yet now before an altar of wrinkles and stillness, I realize there are only a few *agains* allowed us all. Let's not call this death but a soul working its way out of the bone labyrinth—its blind alleys and frantic passageways.

G-MEN IN THE PINES

There were G-men in the pines
as he waited—stiff, leather

glove, white uniform, 32
oz. aluminum bat—for her;

waited for the opportunity to
nick the fence, bruise the bases,

move the crowd. Somebody's
7 p.m. She always drove him

in the wagon, to the diamond,
to the bragging of his outfit.

It was a strong day. Chamomile
sun fidgeting in a high sky;

Mrs. Ackerman kvetched on a bench
while conflicts arose between his ego

and the truth of standing in
front of the building, waiting.

Seven evergreens flanked him. Absent
-eyed, she said, "There are G-men

in the pines. That's why I'm late."
But mom, I don't see anything?

"Forget about the game:
your life is dangling."

SAD, BUT TRUE: A DUET

Write something
beautiful for me.
I need you
 to hurt   *me*
      first.

TRUTH IS

after Jeff Allen's Saturday Blues

Truth is: his pinky no
saga of blood and flesh:
graphite, hickory. Bone
shaved by a pencil sharpener.
Blade: cold-blooded, still.
His finger whittled by a dunce
cap; digit twisted, cranked,
but soon sharp as an Easter
                         suit.

You want someone
to share your vittles.
Your table a flop
house; your tea
spoon: a bent window.

Truth is: clock ain't nothing
but chaos gussied up
and incarcerated. *9:30:*

he drop by, drop draws:
remember glans penis just
a knob with a leaky keyhole:
a 2-for-1 offer: hard: chowder;
limp: pumpkin spit; two wets:
one exit. And he just left
the little boys' room.

                        Upset
and arched, his right eyebrow
a rainbow: his skin: wrinkled
sky. Time's having a hard time
flying tonight. But if his brow
was half a 'stache—like he half
a man—and he were so reclined,
he just might lickle your chippy
hole; might conjure some sweet
                and sour sauce.

10ish: but his fists just bony magnolias
angry at June and its humid libido.

Truth is: life's hard when it ain't
nothing but an oneiric rucksack
chafing daybreak. *11:15*: he
got a chest beige and bumpy
as a country road your tongue long
to mosey on. When he ex and in
and *haling* things, his chest's sink
and swell have your tongue walking
on corduroy water. *Round Midnight:*

Lord's exhausted, snoring. You
check the heavens, edit some
of tomorrow's unpublished edges;
truth is, you peering in Yahweh's
maw; truth is, stars ain't nothing
but the bucked teeth of G-d.

PART II

First they came for the communists and I did not speak out because I was not a communist. Then they came for the trade unionists and I did not speak out because I was not a trade unionist. Then they came for the Jews and I did not speak out because I was not a Jew. Then they came for me and there was no one left to speak out for me.

—Martin Niemoller

MEDIUM EVENING

The *offiziere* commence to soup
and prayer. And as both a dinner
guest and Waffen SS, one *offizier*
tastes Myrna's breast milk in a tureen
of vichyssoise. I had adored the relent
-less engine of Myrna's spirit.

How she twirled even when she
toiled in this dining room where
I tune my viola and truckle before
an Aryan who is leftover ambrosia,
which breaks every bone in the tongue.
An Aryan who insists I play *Gloomy*

Sunday: a Hungarian melody
that stinks deep in the skin.
To pierce the living, I sink
my nails high into my viola's
fingerboard, near the scroll, close
to his throat. To honor the dead,

I play with him—and for him—
on this crippled instrument;
I want to crush the moan in his
Adam's apple: the one given to
him by Myrna. A woman he could
diddle but never love because

her nipples spoke Yiddish. G-d
if I have the power this son
of a bitch will kill himself. So
I play the melody over and over.
      A
fuel, a dust, a gas I dub the speech

of angels. *Noch einmal,* he
insists. I am doing everything
I can to kill this man who teeters
to the balcony and vomits lager
and Myrna's breast milk from his
pores. Doubled over, he reaches

into his back pocket for something
glinting, warm; brandishes a jack
knife and peels the harvest moon
off the roof. Now the sky's lights
are low; and stars find it hard to live
alone because love is gravity for those

who cannot pinpoint the heart.
Autumn, medium evening;
From the east, the welkin
insists: *it might be milky,*
but it is the only way. So
he leans his pistol against

his temple; and I play. He cocks
the hammer; and I play. He pulls
the trigger so hard: it pops! I stop.
The commanding *offizier* growls,
Was ist passiert? Orders me to clean
the mess the SS made of his life.

The hole in his skull: reasonable.
I could see Pegasus out of the side
of his head. *Fait accompli,* I sit
my viola on the balcony: September
        fingers
                              its strings.

FOOL'S GOLD

It was six weeks of briefcases
stacked as high as the tower of Babel.

It was the way a question tastes
when no one knows the answer.

We were—Lonshein, Herzbaum, Chabinsky
and myself, Mordecai—four

jewelers squatting on the floor
in the basement of a warehouse.

We were the private eyes of a storm
we hoped would pass. It was high

windows and slow at first holding
gold, or a cat's-eye, in my right hand.

It was the hum and click of
the SS's boots, which convinced

my muscles that once the fingers learn
to sing memory is just a melody

that will always fuss
in the knuckles. Then

it was fast: weighing a diamond
that had fifty-eight faces: none

of which I recognized. The way old
gold moans: broaches, lorgnettes,

children's rings. Children, yes
my heart was holding its breath

in someone else's mouth. Still
in all it was just that quick

silver: Passover platters, candelabras,
yad pointers. It was monogrammed

suitcases. I swear it was all packed
in large, wooden crates labeled:

SS Reichsfuhrer Berlin. They needed
us to appraise the sparkling juice

of the European Jew. But one suit
case tripped and shattered like a crab

and out of it came a Dead Sea
of gold teeth, the low point, a place

where the earth was too proud
to let me know what hurt.

So I had to push my fist
down Herzbaum's throat

to reason with my own screams. A thousand
mouths demanded I throw my grading

stone through any window. So
these bicuspids and incisors,

these molars and canines, they
began to dance; they began

to howl. We were trapped
in a humid stew, a tornado

of sweet corn kernels
whirling and peeling

the chapped lips of the walls.
We were the eyes of a storm

that had gone blind with rage.
My people's teeth so close to pure

gold.

BACK SPACE: RETURN
Plaszow, Poland, 1944

I

In the barracks, I am
afraid to speak in my
sleep. Afraid if I lie
supine, the photographs
my mind has taken
of the captain's classified
memoranda, reports—
*have the Czechs not
the SS flog the Slavic
 prisoners*—will spring
from my tongue. Still,
I doze off; an argyle
sock buttoned between
my teeth. Anvil-eyed,
I hope one day my
memories will make
the captain writhe on
his *kishke*. "Linski!"
Wwhmmvvhut?
 "The captain wants
you immediately."

II

Breath hot with August and apricot
brandy, the captain looms over me.
"You knew about or planned to
escape with Gottbaum." I fix
my eyes on a steno pad's faint
lines, take dictation. As time
inches toward those hours—
the inky a.m., the impossibly
early—when the eyes of insomnia
are his and his alone, he paces.
Near his villa's French windows,
broad back to me, he strikes
a match. "What shall we do
with Gottbaum's final breath?"
I look up. Flinch. Blink. Not
even an inch from my right eye,
he puffs a *Meistergeiger*,
which, for an instant, I mistake
for the barrel of the .38 caliber
Gottbaum had secured. When
my eye adjusts, I notice, that
like frightened lice, bits
of tobacco leaf are caked
in the corners of his mouth.
He puffs and drapes
a doily of smoke within
an inch of my other eye.
As I depart, shorthand in
hand, he bellows: "When

you type the list leave room
above my signature for another
name." In that instant, my
eyes feel as if they have
overheated. "Linski!" *That's
MY name!* "Yes. You
have an hour!"

III

In the administration building, before a typewriter, I compose a requiem; lug the alphabet of the soon-dead close to the page, but then my fingers flee. I bring my left hand down in blasphemy onto the fingers of my right. Lice pinch my armpits while I peck at this sheet of paper. If the captain does not murder me due to Gottbaum he will do it due to the 'carbons.' How, over time, my mind became a sheet beneath waxy pigment: grey paper that without much pressure imprisoned information. That's why I was certain my memory would make the captain writhe on his *kishke* and bring about his demise. But now I can only hope thoughts loiter in the air after death. Then, a prisoner might pass by the worried earth where I will lie; and when he breathes deeply, all I've been privy to will be his. Honestly, I sense the only thing my memory will inspire is the earth. It is nearly 3 a.m., and I am almost finished. I will leave a space for my name: *Ryzard, Ryzard Linski.* I will leave a space for someone else to sleep in:

it will be vast.

ELMINA

*Ghana's Gold Coast has now virtually
changed into a pure slave coast.*

—Dutch West India Company
Director Rademacher, 1730

My mouth is crowded by over three
months of memory. How
did I end up cuffed, abducted,
thrust through doors where
darkness envies my skin?

How did I find
my life sandwiched
between hundreds of mumbles,
walls and floors fashioned
from minced seashells and spit.
A branding iron insists

our shoulders must smoke and wilt.
Since what cannot be stored in blood must be
discarded from the body's awful architecture;
we have now, somehow, become Portuguese
feces rotting in this limestone

colon. Is this what happens
to the body as the heart erects
its own citadels of bitterness? Beyond
the darkness, a harmattan winces.

Coffled, one morning, I am dragged to a door—which our
host insists resembles their language's little "n." Peering
out from under the archway of what had to be
a small, awful letter in their alphabet,
I witness the sky's lonely

yolk as it punishes the Gold
Coast; then like slippery, silver
question marks, tuna leap from the depths.
These denizens of the sea are convinced
somewhere in the air is the answer

to why the fishermen have gone missing;
they are convinced that now,
to find grief, they must seek it out: the hook,
the yank, the unknown. The ocean
salivates while we drift away. Why

is my heart being ferried
from its dark, throbbing harbor?
Spoon-fashion, I listen to
the surf bark until the barracoon's
drift whittles it down to a whimper;

then, I tuck a promise behind my wall
eye: one day I will return skipping
over the ocean's snowing,
                      broken
          shoulders.

CABO CORSO

*The keeping of the slaves underground is a good security
to the garrison against any insurrection*
—Jean Barbot, 1690

After the sun's been slammed
   shut, I brace for the night
mares where insane echolalia knifes
   through my limestone palisades.

Once shackled within me, Africans
   had dogpaddled in their own feces
'til it hardened; their bones and bowel
   movements caused my floor to swell

two feet. Today, I try to embroider
   the moans of countless ghosts. Today,
I am a fortress shivering with history.
   Hunched, I nibble the loam

for sustenance, scrounge for earth
   no longer anointed with concern;
today, I long to right myself. Unwilling

   to adopt these horrors, the Atlantic—
a divorced teardrop, slapping
   and slipping from shore—offers
me little solace. These dreams

   are insurrections hollering
down the hallways of my head,
   pummeling every door that looks
as if it hasn't slept in centuries.

THIS MURDERED EARTH

*After the Sweet Briar College Plantation Burial Ground
Sweet Briar, Virginia*

It opens out into emptiness.
A paradise of trees bereft of leaves.
A tattered pink ribbon—frayed scarf around
a rusted rod. A wooden stake—a numb
-er *17* atop it—leveled now.
Even in death the ancestors are not
allowed to claim this murdered earth. After
a day's long, hard light in the cemetery,

I almost spit but swallowed it and held
the piddle born inside my kidneys. Forced
my body's brewery to honor the gone.
A branch sneezes beneath me. Three turkey
vultures row the inverted ocean. These words:
a prayer, a briary sky punctures and frays.

SEALED WITH A KISS

> *The warden cut out and discarded the bodies of our letters, pasted the opening and closing greeting together and gave them to us to prove we got something in the mail.*
> —Sam Sewel, Robben Island Political Prisoner

I know your body does not have a throat,
lemon braids or pearls singing from its penis;

I know your body does not have both hips—
the spleen's ill-will and sadness—or its gall
bladder; I know your body does not have

a sphincter, fists or kidneys bruised like beans;
I now know your body is just a skull,
which thinks and stumbles on twisted ankles.

You see the warden deemed you a nuisance
and gouged your skin with scissors, over and over.

My hands will never know your heart's driving
hammer, your navel's gusty, piddling sway.

All I can fathom from your missive's body
is its head: "Dear Sam," and sprained ankles, "Yours since…

UNIVERSITY OF ROBBEN ISLAND

We shall make this prison a university
—Nelson Mandela

Here, sticks are pens and fingers are pencils.
What's useless is useful: blackboards are carved
in thighs of sand. A limestone cove's our
lecture hall. The john—an uncovered bucket—
holds meals that were thrust from our guts.
Real millet: a memory, which makes our tongues
sink, sag like teeming fish nets. Now we scrounge
for water once kissed by golden grains. A hunger

that's both the brain and body craving victuals.
Blisters bloom in our lungs. The sun is
a sucker punch, a fist perched in the eye.
Protocol and feces waylay the guards.
Within the husk of this misfortune lies
an opportunity. Class is in session.

OUT OF MY SYSTEM

*For a former Apartheid prisoner who now works
as a Robben Island tour guide.*

I can't speak with three other tongues, but one
evening mine was the fourth. I was hurled back

into this cage, released after six months;
no work for six years, 'til an Anglican

priest gave me G-d to sell. I came home twice
to sable snow and ash. I had seven mouths

to feed. The island beckoned me, again.
It winked with lesions and gimlets for teeth.

These days, I whisk keen tourists through my nightmares—
their blunt embrace—and mid-sentence, I bob,

drenched to my dreams in quicksand. The piss of warders
and convicts sparkles on my tongue, my lips;

stings prickle my pores. Guess I had to come
back, work this prison out of my system.

FLIGHT 990

As I flee New York in the pre-dawn darkness,
the radio keeps me company. I am the grief
counselor. When I cross state lines, *WWOR*
disowns me, and the static usurping

the station sounds like a symphony
of Rice Krispies. I had taken the first
leg of that flight where steel and sky
kept their long-standing agreement.

Presently, I am driving to
bobbing suitcases, passports
and loved ones' fragmented
jaws. Any mouth would snap

as caterwauls and yawps
pummeled the tongue,
shattered a castle of teeth.

Family members want me to supply
something: a Rolex, a cufflink, an ear
-lobe. All I have are snippets: a half
-moon paving the sea with white gold,

winds out of the southeast at 10 mph;
a 767 heading northwest, not looking
to start an argument with the stars. I bet
pyramids, mouth-watering as sliced pumpkin

pie, crossed some of those passengers' minds
while someone rubbed a hint of paradise
from the cockpit window and sought
out sable sunshine; as I ease it

from the ignition, my car key
feels enigmatic as an Egyptian
hieroglyph. Now I begin the slow

approach to a garden of one of G-d's
mistakes. Now I must shake
hands with those who want answers.
But my palms are deserts: wide, dry,

shifting sand unaccustomed to life.
When asked, all I am allowed to say
is someone up there made a decision,
(which certainly wasn't unanimous.)

PART III
SONIA'S SUITE

*A six-part panegyric for Sonia Sanchez
on the occasion of her 75th birthday.*

POEM NO. 22

I have lived in tunnels and fed the bloodless fish.
—Sonia Sanchez

Dream: a delta of sleep. A February where teenagers hurl
snowballs—bulbs of light scooped from electricity's wet bed.
Youth explodes like the fizz of shaken soda.
Walk gingerly beside memories you are no longer
acquainted with. Hang up the mackinaw sparkling with winter.
When doubts bang on the cream in your eyes, the mind constructs
new apartments. Pin your stutter in a boysenberry corner under the limp
moonlight of a coalminer's heart. Be still—hear the bluegrass weep.

HAIKU

> After *Like the Singing Coming off the Drums:*
> *I am a carnival of stars*
> —Sonia Sanchez

Gave you my shoes so
you could blister with a day's
worth of my walking.

    The sun didn't set
    that was just the sky donning
    a dark sombrero.

A day of dreaming
rubbing up against an eve-
ning's pink emptiness.

    There's a country bake-
    ry decorated by the
    warmth of your hello.

BLUES

> *I'm a Dr. of bluesology. Put a "ology" on what I do
> and become a consultant.*
> —Gil Scott-Heron

Your come on made me go off.
Said your jive time come on made me go off.
Made me scream so loud my pinky toe started to cough.

You swore my love was a bacon, lettuce
and tomato, and you had me sandwiched.
Swore on your life my love was a double

egg and cheese, and you had me sand
wiched. You sink them buck*teeths* in
me you best to get a ambulance.

You had ordered me, but I didn't know I was on the menu.
Wanted the day's special; didn't know I was on the menu.
Then, you asked for free delivery and a bowl of nooky soup.

I've been down so long I must've been afraid of heights.
So low for so long must've been afraid of heights.
Croissant? Paris? Baby, I'm allergic to transatlantic flights.

RIME ROYAL

> After *Does Your House Have Lions:*
> *come down and I will defend your skin*
> —Sonia Sanchez

Sister's Voice

Anger is a city he has always lived in
to try to forget the *xy* denial
from Father—the former capital of his skin.
He sniffed gutter glitter, auctioned his smile.
Under disco balls, lassoed music, stayed awhile.
Bartered for lust when his heart was in hock,
come the night, shut the day at the erotic pawn shop.

Brother, come visit my city where liberty's fractured:
your blood a bell of ebony and ache.
When hate makes few hospitals my arms are an answer.
When the canker on your lips still craves
randy mannequins and third legs without faces,
I will force this malady to its quarantined knees,
make it crawl from your chromosomes; whisper: leave.

Brother's Voice

Sister, hate is a church where our father is not in heaven:
ecumenical fingertips eager for innocence.
Minister's lullabies fondled me at seven.
The Crisco Disco: a temple for the unrepentant,
where I maximized on minimize and found answers in inches.
Father: ever the tourist far from my bones-
holder of tickets allergic to home.

I was experiment—Petri dish, invention.
Father's quarantined Janus.
The something from nothing born of bent intentions.
So I banished his breath, became hedonism's phoenix;
and soared without ire or embers of his penis.
I covet the smirk in palms scarred by diamonds
while sideways I slip through tendrils of silence.

Father's Voice

Maine to Miami: the east coast was the silhouette of a saxophone.
The music that came from it: I made it, chased it.
Son, you turned your tongue to testosterone,
after I'd sunk my solo in gals' lower mouths—made 'em play it.
How do you succumb to something that ain't even named yet?
As my eighth decade encroaches, I kneel in your weak light.
Got an uneasy feeling you'll be the first to say good night.

You ask *why* and my tongue blinks.
But I try to step out of my story:
the who, what, the when, where, the let me think.
My absence from your growing up? Touring?
All answers just empties when you break bread with glory.
I pissed on the past. But could a trace of tomorrow be sutured?
Could I be your student? The dust of your dirge my tutor?

POEM NO. 35

> After *I've Been a Woman:*
> *Under her peace, I know beauty*
> —Sonia Sanchez

You made every inch

of my skin a vacation

I always wanted to take.

Days later, you

echoed in my *everywhere*.

Your sweet sound

and its tangy salvation

lodged in my throat.

But at some point we fell

more in love

with the bluff than each other.

Each of us

with one eye an inch above

the hand we played.

Now without is what we are:

a cool, unusual

punishment. Who drew

this shade across

my heart? And why have you

lead

the rain to this unreasonable

conclusion?

NORMA & BUBBA

> *In a country without age or memory*
> —Sonia Sanchez

Bubba: gangbanger, handball champ, panther black, if anybody messed with me-my St. Nicholas Avenue shank. One day squeezing a handball, Bubba confided in me, (me whose tongue was always tied above untied saddle shoes; me who kept myself at low tide—so there'd be less of me to mess with.) Bubba confided in me that he speaks to leaves.

Norma: in 8th-grade French and algebra—could teach teachers parlez vous AND *par-lez-nomials*. High school. Bubba dropped out, unleashed pimp-limp, do-rag *nigranometry* on 145th. Norma—booted. Could have expelled her swelling belly, but left her brain where it belonged—at the head of the class. French; Outside; Inside; Last. Both heard 'bout my relationship; that it was serious; me and Hunter—the college. I'd heard kids: Norma's quartet; Bubba's trio. By then, I'd amputated my relationship with the neighborhood. Its faces: stubborn stains, washed and forgotten. By then, words were four walls I'd built around me; a library denying my old life access. (Didn't know I had been educated 'til I was erased.) Graduated. Returned a foreigner to myself. Bumped into Norma. The whites of her eyes were piss-filled, yellow toilets. *Hunter, huh?* Sumtin' to do, I shrugged. Played it down; played it dumb; like Lassie, played it dead—pretended Durkheim and Proust weren't growling in my head. *Shoulda been you,* she itched.

Bubba squeezed non-leafy green from me. (They'd both been hanging out with the neighborhood's newest immigrant.) Tracks on all they limbs: I knew where those trains were headed. I headed in the opposite direction. "Later, Bubba." He nodded; I nodded;

he nodded out, and I knew not to do that again. Months later, 18 stories of air abandoned Bubba; somebody wiped my blackboard clean. On it, Norma's spirit snatched the chalk I thought I'd become, reminded me—math was a Romance language. Cold sweat reflected *in* the dark surface, Bubba's ghost served an ace, a corner-killer that ricocheted off that black tar, and St. Nicholas Ave came roaring at me. Tried to duck. Too late. To the world—Bubba, Norma—no need to solve their equations, think about factors. To the world they were just inner-city parentheses loud with emptiness.

PART IV

*Nothing records the effects of a sad life
so completely as the human body.*
—Naguib Mahfouz

AS IF JOY

> *What did I know of love's austere and lonely offices?*
> —Robert Hayden

I
Sundays he took the 28 bus from Blvd and Bartow
to Gun Hill and Fish, the 5 train to Franklin
where splayed on the top floor of a dog-day
row house lay his oldest: a sad sack Lazarus
who could not be resurrected from the bed.

Sundays, he lugged a bag full of victuals
and a mind full of thoughts about his oldest
who resented his father for showing up or resented
himself for being down on a crumb-crowded
mattress doing nothing with his life not even

living it. But from the trudge of his father's
body, a tub of potato salad and a week's
worth of whiting wrapped in paper towels
so oily the fish looked like they had peed
on themselves, the stairs would growl and pop.

II
After the father plumped the fridge with Chips
Ahoys and the pissing fish, he and his
fettered echo, teetered between his
sounds and his son's silence. A TV's

sullen, blue light rippled in the father's
eyes while he clasped his son's left hand
in his right. In that bedroom's dull Sunday
darkness that father's palm: a golden,

warm beef patty. But there was once
a different darkness. This son no
more than ten but more than twenty
minutes late for curfew. This father,

hunched on the punctured couch, fumed
like a jalopy's tailpipe. This son would
toss a soft hello into the living room's ink-
black air. The father's silence: a hatchet.

Now this father would do anything to
dislodge that same brutal tool from his son's
tongue: that lump for bread and utterance
crumpled and indefinitely stunned. But

silence engenders its own whys: *Granny
would say dawn comes after darkest
night,* this father swore then prayed until
his oldest thought his dad's tongue might

faint. Was this father summoning
the duppy of his great granddad—
itinerant preacher, 6'6 maroon—who
had skirted slavery and escaped to the *Land

of Look Behind*? This father who had spun gigs
under Granny's Star Apple Tree. On Standfast
Road as he sat to Sunday's ackee & codfish
—Jamaican scrambled eggs—had this father's

teenage loins, baking beneath that kitchen table, sensed
this future pursued him—a summer of Sundays
leaving meals: nothing spicy, no *Stamp and Go*,
just repasts. Had this father, who on Brown's Town's

The Sudden Country

hills flown kites that would bob and weave
to dodge a gusty wind's sucker punch, sensed
his then unborn, but since crumpled son—who
had bought the orphaned bottles of Old Spice

and *uncuffed* links—would remember the parcel
of years since his father had been pierced
by St. Ann's air. This son bought his father
                            an open-ended Air

Jamaica ticket for his 60th; a gift for a man
who made a life from denying his own; a man
who should be free to watch doctor birds
or women—with Otaheitie and jackfruit

baskets perched atop their heads—
walk as if their noggins were braided
ponds; their wicker baskets: canoes
docked and bobbing above them.

Believing his father would lug him
home in his heart's troubled cargo
hold, as he had lugged vittles to him
with his hands' battered shadows,

this son hoped a DC-9 would whisk
his father to memories empty of cities
that kissed him with balled fists. One city
where this man found himself saying

when he left his oldest on those
Sundays, *look up* as if joy was just
a definition in the dictionary his son
had forgotten the meaning of.

NOSEY

Plump and lonely as a peeled
Idaho potato, my father's nose
hunched between his cheeks.
His nondenominational nostrils

permitted whiffs of honeysuckle
and booboo to worship side by side.
I moped in the bathroom mirror
and feared that genetics' *Manifest*

Destiny would conspire to
stretch my nose into a sugarless
wad of mahogany *Hubba-Bubba
Bubble Gum*. At 13, my beak already

resembled a honking cross
town bus that had crashed
into my cheeks: nostrils scooped,
wide and dark as busted tail lights.

But the rest of my face was
a chalet: bedroom eyes
the color of fava beans.
The dimple in my chin:

a comma. Still, I wanted
to blink and scatter the calm
surface of the mirror. I
wished my reflection were

an echo that careened off the toilet
seat, slid down the bathtub drain,
vanished. I just wanted the mirror
to stop lying to me in the morning

when my eyes were filthy with dreams.
I wanted a nose like Shaun Cassidy's, pert
and blasé as a Chihuahua's. I wished
my face were a blackboard. I'd erase

my instructor's foozle: but I was
taught never to correct my professors.
So as my Oral-B toothbrush tickled
the spit between my teeth, I weighed

my options: duck and imagine a more
endearing self-portrait on this glass
canvas, or continue to cringe, since only
two things fit in this frame: nothing

or *ooogly*. I compromised and packed
my nostrils into a bobby pin: my very
own crinkle-cut, French fry clamp. Now
my nose no longer waddled like a biscuit

-brown storm cloud.

SWEET 16: CHOATE

A New England. Sky-blue
blood trickled into my way
of thinking. But I was more
Boogie Down than boarding
school; more polyester than Polo;
more LL Cool J than LL
Bean. Still, I had come here
to revise the first few chapters
of my life between the soft
covers of this high school's

U.S. history book; I had come
here to doodle. I had not
come here to be smooched
by butternut smiles. I did not
want to be wanted; I just wanted
straight A's: a lonely alphabet
with one other letter—varsity.
Rhonda wanted the chase;
wanted French kisses to smother
the earth—six continents

of scar tissue, nappy patches
of farmland, a broken heart
adrift in space. She was every
afternoon, and it was hard. I was
having a hard time staying hard,
especially with days crowded
by yard markers, thirteen
colonies and tiffs with her. White
and waiting, Susan stood out-
side the locker room macho, invited

me to eat in the dining hall where
Rhonda whispered to the breathless,
the pink and the privileged: *I don't see why
all these white girls like him, he ain't
big.* Maybe when I agreed to Rhonda's
heat, my penis hung at half-mast
because I was crestfallen. And though
Rhonda's words had stung, I never
chowed down with any white guys
and mocked her architecture: her skin's
timid scaffolding; her breast's small cornices.

A week later, Rhonda pleaded: *don't
go out with Susan it'll just be a physical
thing.* That night sitting on my twin
bed, Susan seemed to want something.
Maybe she longed to perform
a duet: black and white notes; brass
and woodwind; no strings attached.
But I ushered Susan out of that evening—largely
because I thought of Rhonda's demons
while clearly she thought little
                         of
                              mine.

17

> *I mus' be about me Faddah's business*
> —Bob Marley

17 notes, lonely and moping, 17 lonely notes timid,
tentative, 17 lonely notes pinched between Bob's
fingers and his Gibson's acoustic strings. Wasn't
with Jamaican nears and dears that I discovered
Nesta. Was Wallingford, where rich kids smoked

cloves, played hackey sack— soccer's impish,
cousin—and ordered *za* with *shrooms*. That deleted
pi sound a gust that could have tautened language's
hammock–the lower lip—where that *mu* could find
refuge. But I guess two extra syllables would have

weighed too much 'pon these kids tongue and teeth.
After curfew, I would slink down to Emile and Pete's
room—a 16th note where I was the darkness that filled
the dot. Sinsemilla smoke undulated like the ruffled hem
of a calico dress. On those illegal evenings, my Park

Avenue chums reacquainted me with myself while they
reasoned 'bout roots Reggae. I listened to them—and Bob
-on their tape deck. Sang along softly, a few words behind:
"Old' Pirates, yes they, Rabbi…" *Rabbi? Gan-Jah Rastafari!*
Bob's not Jewish. It's Rob, I dude. Bob, Rob, they rhyme.

Want a hit? Right then, I imagined pressing my fingers
into sheet music, the staff—a five-stringed guitar, the bar
lines, 19 frets. I would dig my fingers into that paper,
that 19-measure neck, and like the room's smoke, sounds
would rise from that sheet music, dither and stink.

I wish ancestry were an audio cassette I could rewind
six generations to the Scottish buccaneer who wed
a Jamaican woman. Back to where I could fully grasp
that distant union's melody in my body's cells. After all,
my father was the one born four years before Bob

in the same, St. Ann's, Parish. And Nine Mile
was not even nine miles from Brown's Town.
So, why hadn't my mind rescued the Caribbean
side of my mouth? Why was I a sixteenth note
incarcerated beyond this song's horizontal bars?

Honestly, I felt cornered, closed in on by Bob's fret
-board and the staff's five lines. Emile's arrogance
crushing me, but I could not lash out. Was it because
I was more Motown than Island; more Berry than Black
-well; more Marvin Gaye than Reg-gae—the accent always

on the offbeat. I fished the J card of Marley's
Legend from the cassette case. Bob's face reigned
on the cover. Head tilted left, eyes skyward,
right, forefinger curled under his bottom
lip. As if, without that buoy of knuckles,

he feared something might fall
from the white side of his mouth. In
Jamaica, there's a bay called Discovery
where Uncle Sy let me splash in water
as blue as his eyes. Now, huge and salty,

now rippling and bombarded by swimsuits,
one of his orbs became Puerto Seco's waters.
After a dip, I walked on sand white and gritty
as Uncle's hair. But in Wallingford, there was
another bay of discovery that would have mocked

a tale of sitting under the shade of a palm tree's
fronds and feeling as if I were beneath the swollen
shadow of Uncle's eyelashes. Would have cared
less about the sixteen seasons after my last
visit. How time had flown like those four

notes, before the last note, before the first
word of *Redemption Song*. But that 17th
note, like those days during my 17th
year, felt blunt and slow as some
of music's bitter lessons.

PART V

Stop Making Sense
Talking Heads Documentary

MOON IN A BLUE ONCE

The of the cathedral saint of the moon
in a blue once; not snow peas, the eve:
small change and hard times; collard
greens kiss a door knob; soft-shell crab,
the crawl: fire is a candle's applause: the moon
in a blue once; a ginger beer's Eucharist;
love: an out of circulation table
of contents: the dusk of a double
moon; the full cerulean of a die decade;
of a back way when; heaven is a lonely telescope;
an emotional Galileo; a moon in a blue once.
20:12, Mayan Codex; eastern stranded
time: the second/ the month/ the two
moon maiden; a gather up gather up of the then.
Blue years eve. 1883's 1943; Mt. Krakatoa;
the once a once. Tuscany is a cure
for percussion; the sky: a damaged trance;
the moon a tambourine, a poisonous toilet;
each decade: an improvisation; a penitent mask.
Rhythm crumbles into a villa: the sun's flushed
cathedral. Cantata: let the end of the year
leak like a moon in a blue once:
the of the; the of the. *Om.*

SO LITTLE OF HOLLAND

after Claudia Rankine's Provenance of Beauty

Saturday she of the cobalt blue
                          sling, of diablo's arm, of the corn
flesh, of the hair dyed, of the aged
                          middle. "Do you Mother any books
about Theresa?" He of the bald brown,
                          of the sixtyish, of the barrel-bottom gravel,
of the librarian: no was, was stolen. He
                          of the whisper, of the walked away.
Hadn't heard Theresa's name.
                          But an about hour ago Theresa was
not Calcutta but the 70's: The Prospect:
                          an Avenue of the forgotten G-d while I
sat in a sausage with tinted windows;
                          let my life look back at me in lowercase; ear
to ear cantilever speakers. *Contigo, conmigo,*
                          amigo? There is a speak from the lower depths;
a trio of the occasional quartet; cream and crimson
                          NebraskaLand eighteen wheelers that lumber
along the translation of Faile St. A monologue
                          of raw sewage; how a few centuries can be sutured
by petrol and lavalier. Accommodate the oxygen.
                          How it double parks in the nostrils. The Bronx so little
of Holland, the supposed Jonas. An echo of the giddy up
                          and dash. The poor and Pentecostal. The eastern
seaboard and Atlantic rub elbows, soak a few
                          syllables with sleep; abandon the narrator,
turn your back on the I-hear-her-sable because
                          a creative cowboy always
dismounts from 60% of a horse.

THE SHADOW OF LANGUAGE

The language of bubble is twinkle.
    The language of YouTube is sky.
The language of tongue is freelance.
    The language of jelly is per se.
The language of river is Facebook.
    The language of bouillon is patois.
The language of sweat is stinkstone.
    The language of transom is creamy.
The language of moonlight is isinglass.
    The language of amber is Chablis.
The language of penis is eager.
    The language of thought is lonely.
The language of whisper is benzene.
    The language of IPod is fire.
The language of foie gras is kinky.
    The language of breathing is wrinkled.
The language of ink is death.
    The language of satin babbles.
The language of *goo-goo* is *Ga-Ga*.
    The language of you is me.
The language of jasmine is breathless.
    The language of P-funk is chitterlings.
The language of Vivaldi is Sistine.
    The language of pas de deux: cowpoke.
The language of blizzard is kinship.
    The language of skin is nappy.
The language of cocoa is Tuesday.
    The language of Texas is bidet.
The language of zephyr is gingham.
    The language of canyon is toadstool.
The language of heartache is solemn.
    The language of fanzine is toe-jam.

The language of cactus is rayon.
    The language of mustard's seductive.
The language of coral is Atman.
    The language of ham is blind.
The language of zephyr is olio. [ibid]
    The language of field holler: egg yolk.
The language of booboo is Slavic.
    The language of hope is Colgate.
Lightning's language is ontological.
    The language of nipple is misty.
The TV of language is foreign.
    The language of shadow is bliss.
The language of stardust is prayer.
    The language of solstice is Morpheus.
The shadow of language is Sunday.
    The shadow of language is Sunday.
The shadow of language is someday.

PART VI

The tendinous part of the mind, so to speak, is more developed in winter; the fleshy, in summer. I should say winter had given the bone and sinew in literature, summer the tissues and the blood.

-John Burroughs

A PARABLE OF SKILLETS

Jamaica, West Indies

Sand, hard as toast, burns
the balls of my feet.
The sea is an epic I nibble.

Paya and Granny's azure
eyes soak the ocean.
Daddy returns with a skirt:

*Dee, this is Mer'lyn. We grew
up togetha.* It was hard
dough bread and St. Ann's

Parish. The way him fingers drink
her smile. Montego Bay deep. Breathing
in the steam of a crime.

                              Ma
an ocean away frying
chicken: a southern Baptist

limerick: a Eucharist of fingers
and grease. I know something
is wrong. My tongue is

a red hot coal; my words ashes.
But daddy teaches me to close
my mouth one tooth at a time.

RIO DÉJÀ VU NO

Rio De Janiero, Brazil

Kneading Rio's coast,

Dani and I try to pry the sea and sky apart; try
to pinpoint Copacabana's horizon because

a coterie of pickpockets filched midnight's
stars. The Atlantic is ravenous: a black

on black cat who opens its jaws,
foams at the mouth and snarls

one hundred meters from our feet.
Is that merely sand twinkling

in my hair as I eat *Bolinhas
de Bacahlau?* In Dani's and my

dinner conversation one
word—*love*—quivers

like candlelight, and I know
I've been in Ipanema before,

though my lungs have never inhaled
the dust of Botofogo. I turn, hold

out my arm, and a past life
vanishes. Tonight, I am Black

Orpheus. Tonight, I have taken a breath,
deep, from someone else's body.

EASTER IN RIO
Rio De Janiero, Brazil

Come Easter, January is a river plump
with religious fish. Twenty-one
hundred feet above us—hunchbacked,
so as not to nick his pate on a cloud—

Christ stands in soapstone. At cockshut,
Dani and I circle *Favelas* while she snaps
and twirls smoke from her *Marlboro
Light.* Her Nikon needs lithium batteries.

Standing outside a pharmacy, she swears
she is having a déjà vu; swears she'd been
in this drugstore before; before, before
befriended after. She insists the pharmacy's

windows look out onto a church
steeple: windows are memory's
thin enemies. The apothecary
doesn't have batteries. Beyond

one of the store's window
panes, vespers elbow
the air. Rather than talk
about how neither of us
had ever been to Rio,

Dany eases her tongue
inside my mouth
and draws memories
from my tongue until
it is merely a nub
of speechless *linguisa.*

MONDAY'S AT MARTHA'S VINEYARD

Buttered popcorn sky
from the champagne of sunset
the ocean was drunk

ABUELA'S DREAMS
Caracas, Venezuela

Grandma lives alone, but dreams keep
her company. She said she saw me on
a bus adorned with bowie knives and ash.

But I don't ride buses. I breathe in
a country with no name, where
English sleeps in a cheekbone.

In Spanish, none of the letters sit still.
So, in Caracas my tongue is swollen
with the gooey music of song.

The moon is the sun to a drunk
pirouetting, anointed by the curdled
milk of a street lamp. Killing time

with a butter knife, I poke my ideas
into bars. With my kneecaps beneath
a table, I tattoo people's laughter

and ignore the bickering of Christ-
mas. I eventually stumble into
a *camion* to *Capitolio* where six

locals board dressed like a proposal
no one wanted to make. Bowie
knives smirk while these locals

slit purse straps, bag bottoms,
and leap off heavier than they
boarded. Shaken, I know

I have reached *Macuto* when I see
a choker twinkle around
a mountain's ankle; verdant hills

greased with the breath of G-d.
It's then, I remember Grandma
and relish her softest drink: dreams.

As music escorts me to the beach
the next morning, mosquitoes
have me for breakfast. On the shore
I slip off my sneakers, tiptoe on

the glass, the rocks. Three Polar
Beer bottles lean against a broken
arm of towhead driftwood. With my

eyelashes, I long to scratch
the sun out of the sky; nail
the sea to my front teeth;
drizzle home. Instead,

I search for smidgeons
of the Atlantic on your brow
Azuca Negra. Here, a kiss does
not have to look very far for lips.

Here, I want to lick the rhythm
in your knuckles, whisper Pralines
& Cream between your toes: sticky,
cold, yummy, suck. The men tell

me you are no good.
Every night, they sense
a sprained ankle's innuendo
on your nipples. Down

the boardwalk, you fade
like a memory too cruel to
question. Now my pen bleeds

isinglass. A choir croons
a "Little Drummer Boy."
La gente tear the air
with a sign of the cross.
I eye Jesus simmering

in a mug of oolong tea; pray
to Saint Jude who insists
I skinny-dip between
the graffiti of Abuela's dreams.

EL NORTE

Guatemala

Like fingers on a typewriter,
rain pounds the cobblestone.
For the last time, I will tongue

the mud of my country;
the *café con leche*; that
aroma will linger on

my lips forever. One
deep breath and home will
flood my head. I must move,

do not ask me to lie still
and sequester my breath
as it flees my lips. There

they have toilets
that flush. We must
go sister. We must

ask the night not to
nod off and keep
at least one eye

open for the smell of betrayal.
We meet our coyote
who tells us to climb

into a Texan's rancid
culo, a *gringo* who
will vomit us

from his troubled stomach into
the mouth of another America.
We could be two strings of *bistec*

he picks from his teeth. Hours from now,
I will leap from his chapped lips and learn
broken English, which will not break

mi corazon the way you did
when you died, *hermana*.
I will work for my green

card in a restaurant
serving smiles that simmer.
Immigration will

find out, and I will
use my head before
someone cuts it

                off.

NOTES

THE SUDDEN COUNTRY

Standfast: a road in Brown's Town, Jamaica
Brown's Town: a town in St. Ann's Parish, Jamaica (Bob Marley was from St. Ann's Parish)
June Plum: edible fruit also known as the Golden Apple.
Red Stripe: a beer drunk locally
Matterhorns: a brand of cigarettes

In Jamaica they drive on the left side of the road and older car models in the late 70s—still influenced by the British—had cars with the steering wheels on the right side of a car.

Irish Sea Moss: a sweet drink made from Sea Moss a supposed aphrodisiac
WRJR: a Jamaican radio station
"Land of My Birth": 1978 Jamaican hit record sung by Eric Donaldson
Runaway Bay: a town in St. Ann's Parish
Nesta: the middle name of Reggae great Bob Marley
Prime Minister Michael Manley & opposition leader Edward Seaga: leaders of the two, rival leading political factions [the People's National Party (PNP) and Jamaican Labour Party (JLP) respectively] in Jamaica.
In the same year (1978) that Donaldson's "This is the Land of my Birth" was a smash hit, Marley headlined "The One Love Peace Concert," which might have warded off civil war. During his performance, Marley got both Prime Minister Manley and opposition leader Edward Seaga to join him on stage where the rivals shook hands.
"Feel all right": lyrics from the hit song One Love, from which the concert got its name.
"Light throughs" and "lest wes": words from the Jamaican National Anthem.

The Sudden Country

Kiai: the sound a martial artist makes when doing a karate chop.
Perseid: meteor shower that happens in August in the Northern Hemisphere and a byproduct of comet Swift-Tuttle.

PART I

"Three the Hard Way"
Bootyny, Sop De Bottom, Coodemay and Stew Beef are characters in Hurston's novel "Their Eyes Were Watching G-d" who live in the Eatonville, Florida town Hurston uses as the story's setting.

"Illiterate Fish"
Lodz: a city in Poland noted for its film school.
Ni spac: Polish for "don't sleep."

"Block Island Cemetery"
An island off the east coast of Rhode Island in the Atlantic. There is a cemetery of some of the family's of the oldest European settlers. One of those families was the Balls'. My partner and I visited the cemetery in 2009. The first headstone past the entrance was Simon Ball—who shared my birthday. Next to his headstone was that of his wife Celia Ball—her birthday was two days before my partner's. This eerie coincidence prompted me to ruminate on the notion of past lives. My partner has a lithograph of 20th century realist painter Andrew Wyeth's "Christina's World" hanging above her bed. There were times in that room that I felt like she and I were connected in another life and the coincidence at the Block Island Cemetery underscored that feeling.

"The Bone Labyrinth"
rock is urban term for a basketball.

PART II

"Medium Evening"
A melancholic Hungarian ballad that was often sung by lovesick men

or quoted in suicide notes written by men, distraught over love. Both Billie Holiday and Elvis Costello recorded an English version.
Offizier/e: Officer/s.
Gloomy Sunday: a Hungarian song written in 1933, dubbed the 'Suicide Song' because individuals had allegedly taken their lives after listening to the haunting melody, or that the lyrics had been left with their last letters. Its popularity increased through Billie Holiday's 1941 recording of it.
Noch einmal: again.
Was ist passiert?: What happened?

"Fool's Gold"
Cat's-eye: a gem.
Yad pointer: a decorated rod used in a synagogue to indicate the text of the Torah to be read in the day's service.

"Back Space"
Kishke: Yiddish word for gut.
Meistergeiger: A German cigar.

"Elmina and Cabo Corso"
Elmina was the first slave dungeon built during the transatlantic slave trade. It was erected by the Portuguese in 1486. The term, Elmina, means "the mine" because the Europeans/Portuguese initially went to Ghana, West Africa in search of gold, but subsequently trafficked in humans. Cabo Corso—also from the Portuguese language—means "short cape." The Portuguese built the first lodge in Cabo Corso in 1555. The name Cabo Corso was eventually corrupted to Cape Coast, which became the name both of the dungeon and the surrounding town. The Swedes built the first version of the Cabo Corso "fort"/dungeon in 1653. The English rehabilitated the Swedish structure and that is the building someone would encounter today. Elmina and Cabo Corso are located near each other in Cape Coast/ Gold Coast Ghana. Ghana had the ignominious distinction of being the West African kingdom with the most slave dungeons—47—during the transatlantic slave trade.

"Flight 990"
WWOR: a radio station broadcasting to parts of the tri-state area (New York, New Jersey, Connecticut.) This poem is about a plane crash in October, 1999 of an Egypt Air flight that was headed to Egypt from New York. Somebody in the flight crew might have intentionally downed the plane. The poem's voice is of a grief counselor who had actually taken the first leg of the flight, which flew from Los Angeles, landed in New York and then was to continue on to Egypt.

PART III

"Poem No. 22" and "Poem No. 35"
Looking at Sonia Sanchez' oeuvre, I noticed that she would title poems with just a number. And within a given book these poems would not necessarily be in numerical order. So I tried to reflect her aesthetic choice in my numbering of poems in this encomium.

"Rime Royal"
Sonia Sanchez wrote a book entitled *Does Your House Have Lions?* It is a book length elegy—in three voices—to her brother who died of AIDS in the early 80s. She uses the form Rime Royal, which is a seven-line form with an ABABBCC rhyme scheme. The book is framed by three sections, written in the voice of the sister, the brother and the father. I have written two stanzas in Rime Royal to represent each of these voices and their concerns.

PART IV

"As if Joy"
Runaway Bay: town in St. Ann's Parish.
Duppy: ghost.
Maroon: escaped slaves on the island of Jamaica who created their own settlements.
Nanny Town: a settlement that escaped maroons created during slavery—it is in the interior of Jamaica known as Cockpit

Country—and from which they successfully battled the Spaniards and subsequently the British.
Star Apple: an edible fruit.
Standfast Road: the street in Brown's Town where my father grew up.
Ackee & codfish: the "national" dish of Jamaica ackee-fruit that is boiled when cooked; the codfish is sauteed in coconut oil.
Stamp and Go: codfish fritters.
Doctor Birds: a hummingbird so called because the tail feathers look like those old-fashioned doctor's jackets. It is mostly green with a long black tail.
Otaheitie: a fruit that starts out with a green rind which then turns pink then red. It is white inside.
Jackfruit: a big, fleshy, green fruit with a creamy brown inside.

"Sweet 16"
Boogie Down: slang for the Bronx, New York.

"17"
"Za" "shrooms": I went to boarding school and the kids called pizza with mushrooms on it "za" with "shrooms."
St. Ann's Parish: one of the 14 Parishes that make up the island of Jamaica.
Nine Miles: village in St. Ann's Parish in which Bob Marley was born.
Island: the name of the record label Bob signed to.
Berry Gordy: founder of Motown Records.
Chris Blackwell: founder of Island Records, Bob Marley's label.
J card: the material inserted into old-fashioned cassette cases that had artwork, production credits and often lyrics printed on them.
Legend: name of Bob Marley's Greatest Hits album.
"White side of his mouth": Bob Marley's father was a white Englishman named Norval Sinclair Marley.
Discovery Bay: town in St. Ann's.
Puerto Seco: a beach in Discovery Bay.
Redemption Song: a prophetic hit song written by Bob Marley with

a Dylanesque feel.

PART VI

"Easter in Rio" and **"Rio De Ja Vu No"**
Copacabana: beach and zone in Rio de Janiero.
Ipanema: beach and zone in Rio de Janiero.
Botofogo: beach and zone in Rio de Janiero (all three of these zones are contiguous).
Bolinhas de Bacahlau: Codfish balls—the fish prepared into round meatball shaped bits and eaten.
January: the literal translation of Rio De Janiero is "River of January."
Favelas: the slums on the hills of Rio de Janiero made famous in the Oscar-winning film "Black Orpheus.'
Linguisa: Portuguese sausage, a staple in Brazil.

"Abuela's Dream"
Abuela: grandmother.
camion: a small bus.
Capitolio: a section of Caracas.
Macuto: a seaside Venezuelan town.
la gente: the people.
azuca negra—black/brown sugars

"El Norte"
Culo: behind.
Café con leche: Coffee with milk.
Bistec: beefsteak.
Hermana: sister.
Coyote: trafficker in undocumented immigrants.
Corazon: heart.

With Thanks

Mom and Dad for loving and letting, Uncle Frank, Apple, Layding, rara, Cuz, Grandma Elaine, T&T (Tim & Terrance), Phyllis (the portal), Glen, Jeff, John Al, Uncle Harold, Doctor, DJ, M. Scott, Carol F, Monika, my sands, TLC, Pat, Ilka, Howard, DSM, Ashby and Langston Hughes—my poetic guardian angel.